The Constellation Cassiopeia

Lisa Owings

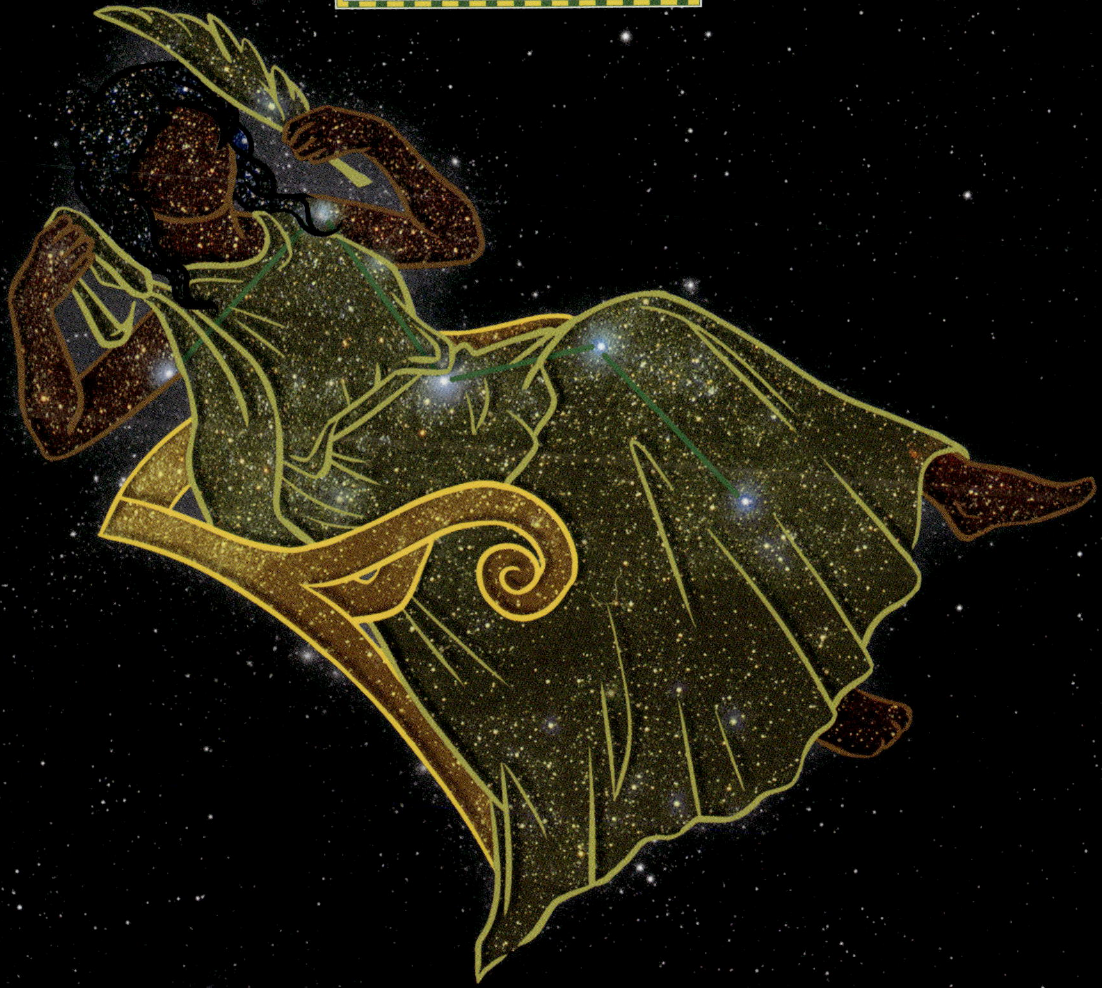

Published by The Child's World®
800-599-READ • www.childsworld.com

Photography Credits
Photographs ©: Shutterstock Images, cover (illustration), cover (background), 1 (illustration), 1 (background), 2 (illustration), 2–3 (background), 5 (illustration), 7, 17, 18, 22, 29; E. Slawik/NSF/AURA/M. Zaman/NOIRLab, cover (constellation), 1 (constellation), 2 (constellation), 5 (constellation); NASA, 8, 9; iStockphoto, 11; Johannes Hevelius/Barry Lawrence Ruderman Antique Maps Inc., 13; Pictorial Press Ltd./Alamy, 14; Jeremy Alan Baxter/Shutterstock Images, 21; Annibale Carracci and Domenichino/Farnese Gallery, 25; Fedor Selivanov/Shutterstock Images, 27; Design elements from Shutterstock Images

ISBN Information
9781503875784 (Reinforced Library Binding)
9781503876200 (Portable Document Format)
9781503876828 (Online Multi-user eBook)
9781503877320 (Electronic Publication)

LCCN 2025938258

Printed in the United States of America

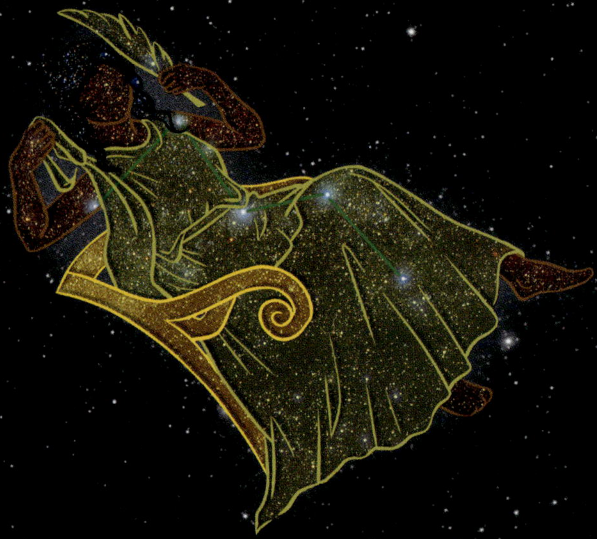

ABOUT THE AUTHOR

Lisa Owings has a degree in English and creative writing from the University of Minnesota. She has written and edited a wide variety of educational books for young people. Lisa lives in Andover, Minnesota, where Cassiopeia is in the sky every night.

TABLE OF CONTENTS

CHAPTER ONE

The Constellation Cassiopeia

The night sky is like a window to the **universe**. Through it, people can see stars shining brightly in the darkness. Since **ancient** times, people have traced pictures in the stars. These pictures are called constellations. People tell stories about the constellations. One of these stories is about a lovely but **vain** queen. The ancient Greeks gave her the name Cassiopeia (kass-ee-oh-PEE-uh). The outline of the seated queen looks like a W or an M depending on the time of night and time of year. Cassiopeia is often upside down on her **throne**.

Stars are bright balls of hot gas. The hottest stars are blue. Other stars are slightly cooler. They can be white, yellow, orange, or red. Some stars are the size of a city. Others are many thousands of times larger than Earth. The brightest stars can be seen from trillions of miles away. Cassiopeia has some of the brightest stars in the night sky.

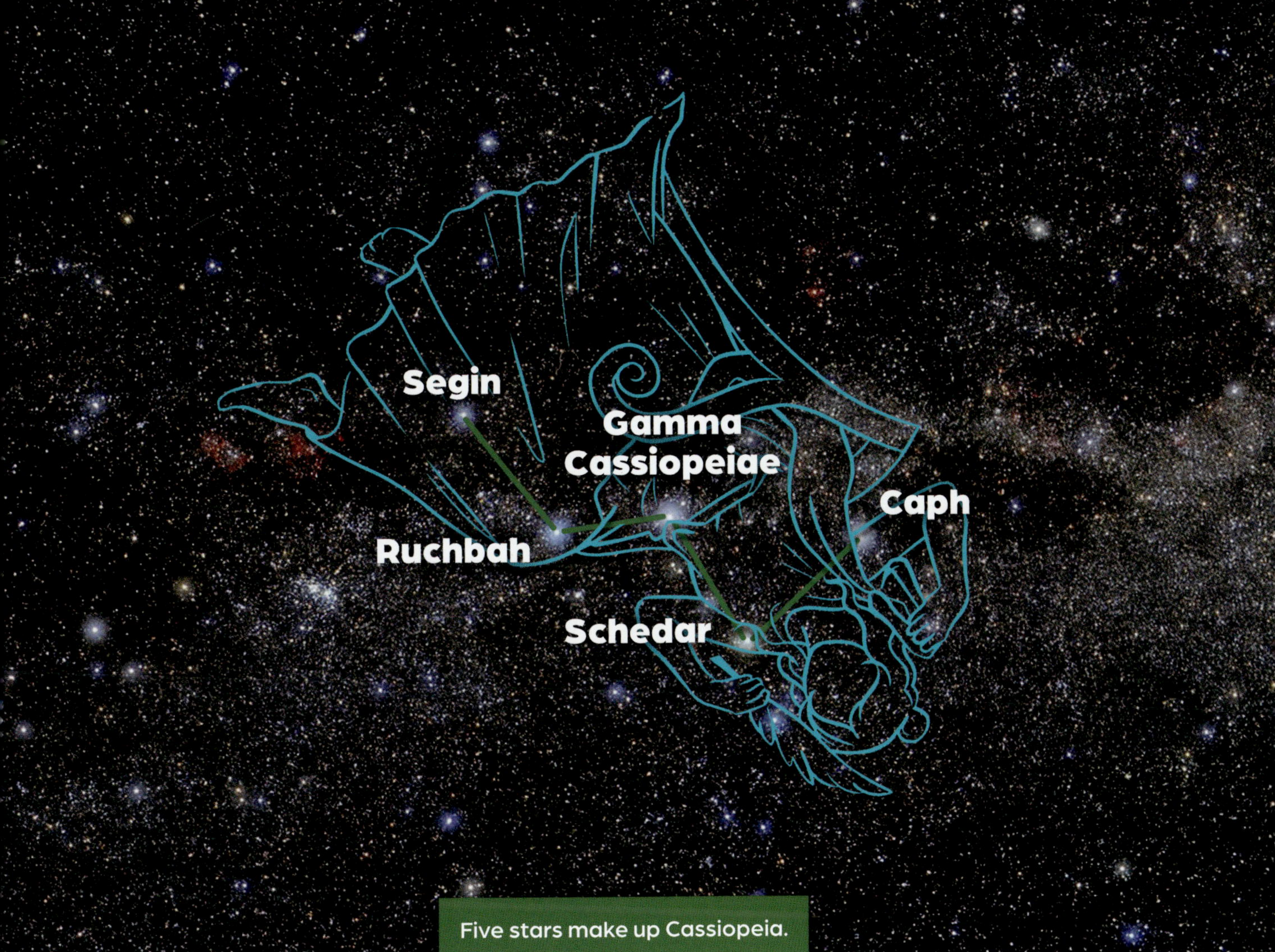

Five stars make up Cassiopeia.

Cassiopeia's W is made up of five stars. Segin is the constellation's faintest star. It marks Cassiopeia's leg and one end of the W. The first zig leads to Ruchbah. *Ruchbah* means "knee." The star marks Cassiopeia's knee. The next zag leads to Gamma Cassiopeiae, the middle star. The next zig in the W leads to Schedar. This giant orange star is the constellation's brightest star. It sits at Queen Cassiopeia's chest. At the end of the W is the white star Caph.

Cassiopeia's throne is set against the Milky Way. This is Earth's **galaxy**. The Milky Way galaxy is a bright disc-shaped spiral. Bands of the Milky Way are visible from Earth. A band stretches deep into space behind Cassiopeia.

The Milky Way is home to many star clusters. These groups of stars are held close together by **gravity**. They can be seen through a telescope or binoculars. There are star clusters in Cassiopeia. One cluster is called M52. It is a dense cluster of stars. A line drawn from Schedar through Caph points to it. The M103 cluster near Ruchbah has a huge red star at its center. NGC 7789 is another colorful cluster in Cassiopeia.

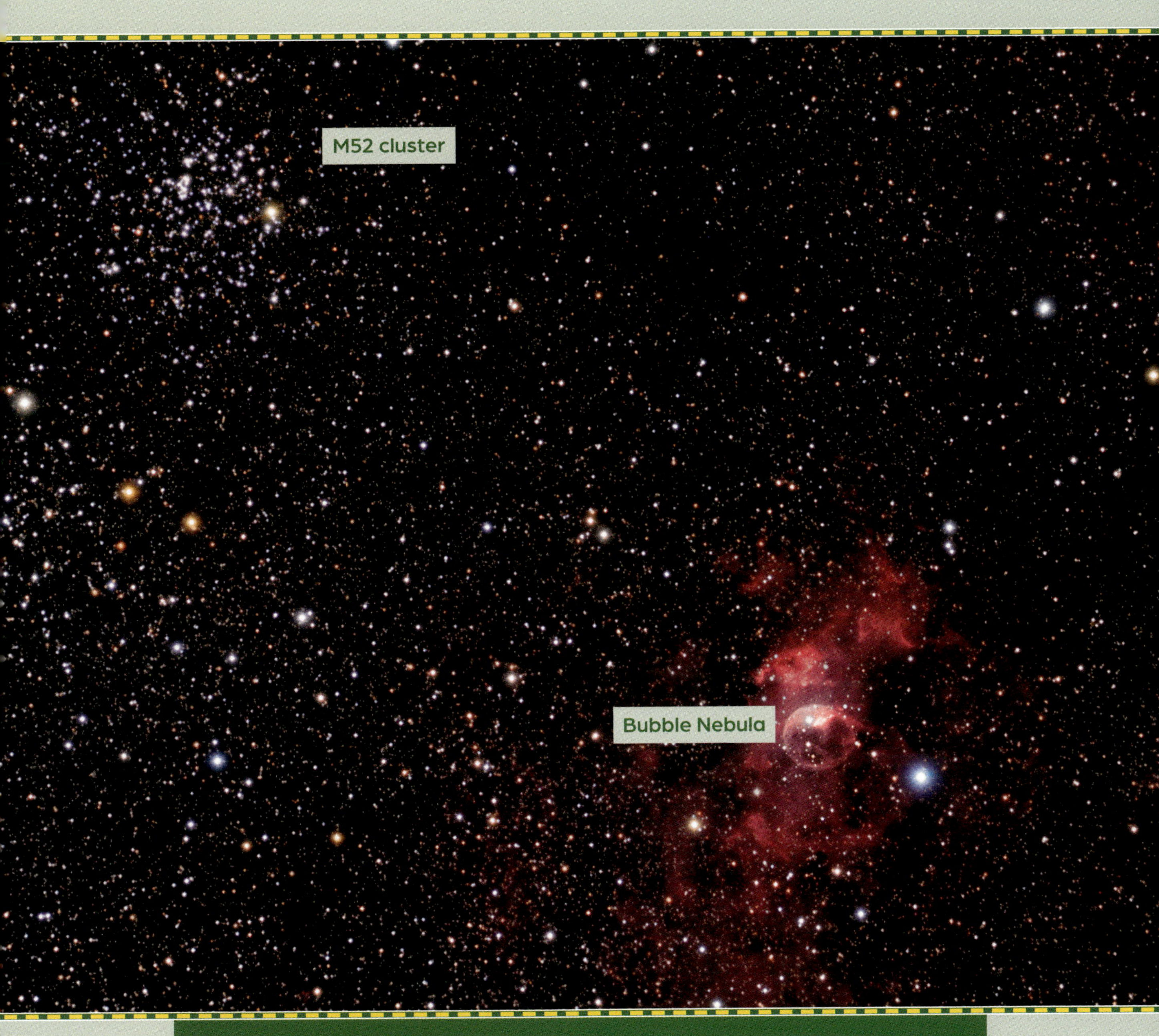

The M52 cluster is near NGC 7635. This object is known as the Bubble Nebula. A star is being born inside this nebula. The gas gets so hot that it forms a bubble.

The Andromeda Galaxy is named for Cassiopeia's daughter, Andromeda.

Countless other galaxies lie beyond the Milky Way. Two of them are found in Cassiopeia. The half of the W tipped by Schedar points to galaxies called NGC 147 and NGC 185. This small pair of galaxies moves around the larger Andromeda galaxy.

Cassiopeia does not move through the skies alone. She is surrounded by her family. The starry image of her husband, King Cepheus (SEE-fee-yus), is forever at her side. Also nearby are her daughter and son-in-law, Andromeda and Perseus. In the Northern **Hemisphere**, these constellations are all in the sky on winter nights.

There are 88 official constellations in the night sky. Around AD 150, Greco-Roman **astronomer** Ptolemy (TAH-luh-mee) wrote a book. He described 48 constellations. Most of these are part of today's constellations. Other constellations were added in the 1600s and 1700s. In the 1900s, scientists drew official borders around the constellations. They divided the sky into 88 areas with no space in between. This means every star seen from Earth is part of a constellation region.

SUPERNOVAS

Stars are not living objects. But they still have life cycles. Stars are born in clouds of dust and gases. They burn for billions of years. Some giant stars die in huge explosions called supernovas. A supernova is blindingly bright and beautiful. The remains of some supernovas can be seen in Cassiopeia. A famous one is Cassiopeia A. This star exploded in the 1600s. A line drawn from Ruchbah through Gamma Cassiopeiae points to it. Little is still visible of Cassiopeia A. But it still sends out lots of X-ray waves and heat.

Cassiopeia A

CHAPTER TWO

The Origin of the Myth

People traced patterns through Cassiopeia's stars long before Ptolemy's time. It may have been known as Cassiopeia as early as 3500 BC. Several ancient cultures recognized the W shape of Cassiopeia. But each imagined the stars to represent something different. Arabs saw a hand, a camel, or a dog. The Chinese saw horses and a **chariot**. The Celts saw the palace of a fairy king. Ancient Greeks first saw a key. It was not until later that Cassiopeia became a queen.

The ancient Greeks told the story of Queen Cassiopeia. But they likely borrowed her name and parts of her story from another culture. Experts disagree on where the myth of Cassiopeia was first told. It may have come from the Middle East or India.

People have seen patterns in Cassiopeia's stars throughout history.

Greek astronomer Eudoxus lived in the 300s BC. He was the first Greek known to write about Cassiopeia and other constellations. But his work would be lost if it were not for the Greek poet Aratus. Aratus turned Eudoxus's writing into a poem. This poem is all that survived of Eudoxus's work. Aratus described Cassiopeia as seeming unhappy. Other Greek and Roman writers retold Cassiopeia's story in the following centuries. Some stories say Cassiopeia was from Aethiopia, a region in northern Africa. Some say she was a queen in the Middle East. Each writer told the story a little bit differently. But the main ideas were always the same.

In the Greek story, Cassiopeia bragged about her beauty. The sea god Poseidon wanted to punish her for her pride. He sent a sea monster to destroy her kingdom. The only way for Cassiopeia to save her people was to **sacrifice** her daughter Andromeda to the monster. Perseus rescued Andromeda. But Poseidon wanted to be sure Cassiopeia had learned her lesson. He tied her to her throne. Then he set her in the sky as a constellation. He made sure Cassiopeia tipped uncomfortably upside down as she circled the heavens.

Sometimes Cassiopeia is upright in the sky. But she is often upside down or sideways.

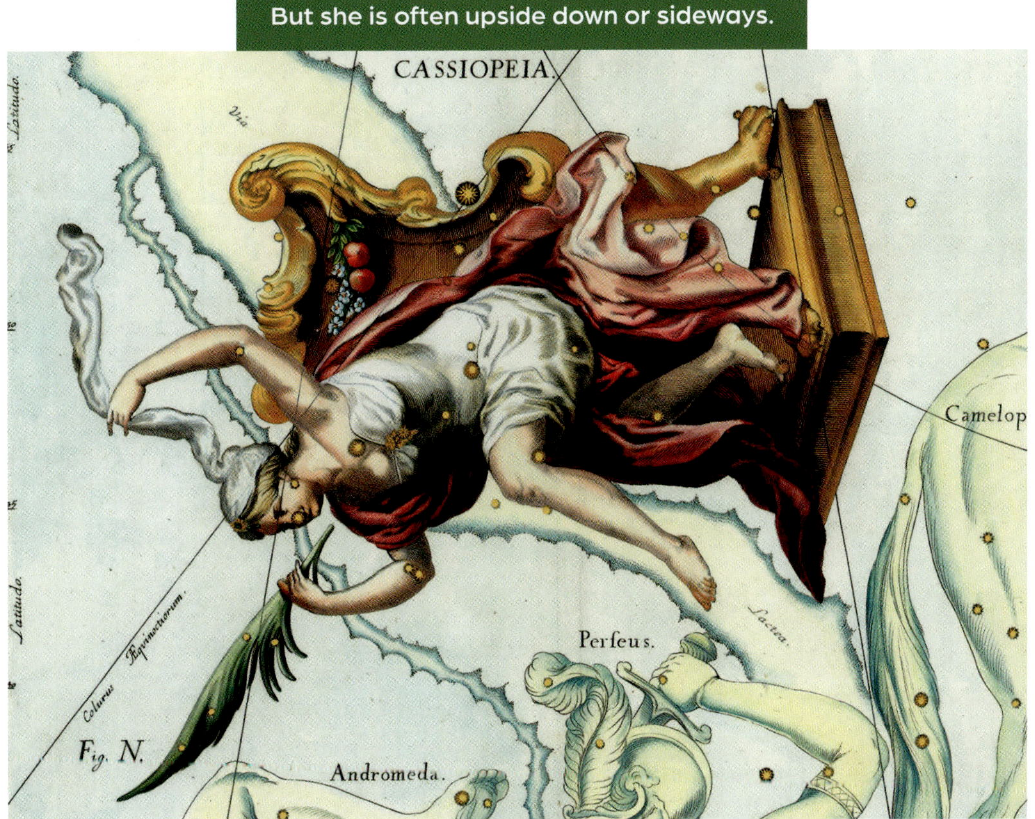

The movie *Clash of the Titans* (1981) tells the story of Perseus and Andromeda. It was remade in 2010.

The story of Cassiopeia served as a lesson for the Greeks. Cassiopeia was too proud. She placed herself and her daughter above the gods. Greek people believed this kind of pride brought punishment from the gods. Her bright stars were a constant reminder to be **humble**.

The story of Andromeda was also important to the Greeks. Andromeda was an innocent beauty. She almost lost her life because of her mother's vanity. But the hero Perseus saved her at the last moment. This classic story was very popular among the Greeks. Perseus became a beloved hero in Greece and around the world. Many artists have painted the daring rescue of Andromeda. Plays and operas tell the story of Cassiopeia's family.

CHAPTER THREE

The Story of Cassiopeia

Queen Cassiopeia was very beautiful, and she was proud of her beauty. Cassiopeia's daughter, Andromeda, was even more beautiful than her mother. Andromeda was engaged to be married.

Cassiopeia was as proud of Andromeda's beauty as she was of her own. The queen could not resist boasting. One day, Cassiopeia's pride got the best of her. She bragged that she and Andromeda were more beautiful than the sea nymphs, spirits of the ocean.

The vain queen's words drifted over the nearby sea. They soon reached the sea nymphs' ears. One of the nymphs was Amphitrite, wife of the powerful sea god Poseidon. The sea nymphs were furious! They went to Poseidon. They told him what the queen had said. Poseidon listened to their words. His anger quickly grew. He promised to punish Cassiopeia for her vanity.

Poseidon is the Greek god of the sea. He is known as Neptune in Roman mythology.

Cassiopeia and Cepheus did not want to lose their daughter.

Poseidon sent a flood with a fearsome sea monster to destroy Cassiopeia's kingdom. She and King Cepheus were horrified when they learned of this threat. Cepheus had to do something to save his kingdom. He visited an **oracle** for advice. But the advice was not what Cepheus wanted to hear. The oracle said there was only one way to save their kingdom. Cepheus and Cassiopeia had to sacrifice their only daughter to the hungry sea monster.

Cepheus could not bear the thought of Andromeda being eaten. But his people convinced him he had no choice. They forced him to chain Andromeda to a rock, where she was pounded by waves. She lay helplessly in the sea monster's path. It would not be long before the evil creature came and swallowed her. Cepheus and Cassiopeia looked on fearfully. Andromeda wept. There was nothing for her to do now but accept her cruel fate.

Just then, a man flew overhead. Wings on his sandals carried him through the air. His name was Perseus. He was a son of the mighty Zeus, king of the gods. Perseus had just beheaded the Gorgon Medusa. Gorgons were creatures with snakes for hair. Medusa's gaze could turn people to stone.

Perseus looked down at Andromeda. The weeping princess was too beautiful. He could not leave her. Perseus was in love. He landed near her and asked why she was chained. Andromeda told him what had happened. But her words trailed off in a scream. The sea monster's scaly head was rising over the waves!

PERSEUS AND PEGASUS

In some versions of the myth, Perseus rides a winged horse when he saves Andromeda. This horse was Pegasus. Pegasus was born from Medusa's blood after Perseus beheaded her. The horse was originally associated with the hero Bellerophon. But Perseus was a more popular hero. Over time, the stories of Perseus and Bellerophon got mixed up. Perseus became associated with Pegasus.

Perseus rescued Andromeda from the sea monster.

Perseus quickly flew over to Cassiopeia and Cepheus. He said he would try to rescue their daughter. But he made them promise him something first. If he saved Andromeda, she had to marry him. Andromeda was already engaged. But the king and queen agreed. They wanted their daughter saved. Just before the monster reached Andromeda, Perseus flew high into the air. The sea monster saw Perseus's shadow on the waves. Perseus dove from above as the monster attacked his reflection. He plunged his blade deep into the creature's flesh, cutting off its head.

Perseus gently released Andromeda from her chains. Then it was time to celebrate. A wedding feast was held for Perseus and the princess. But the splendid event was soon spoiled.

Andromeda's fiancé, Phineus, stomped in. He brought his army with him. He ordered Andromeda to marry him instead of Perseus. A battle took place. Perseus fought bravely. But he was no match for Phineus's large army. Luckily, Perseus still had Medusa's head. He told the princess to close her eyes. Then he pulled the head out of his bag. He held it up for his enemies to see. They all turned to stone! Perseus had saved the day again.

The gods honored Andromeda's family by placing them in the sky as constellations. But Poseidon was still angry at Cassiopeia. He bound her to her throne. He set her in the sky at an uncomfortable angle. Forever after, she would move through the skies with her head slanted down.

Storytellers disagreed on whether Andromeda's fiancé was named Phineus or Agenor. No matter his name, Perseus turned him to stone.

CHAPTER FOUR

THE MYTH OF CASSIOPEIA IN OTHER CULTURES

The bright W of Cassiopeia has caused wonder since ancient times. Many cultures have woven their own stories around these stars. Early Arabs saw them as the fingertips of a hand painted with henna. People use this reddish dye to decorate their hands and feet. The designs are said to bring good luck. Other Arabs saw the humps of a kneeling camel in the constellation. Camels were hugely important in Arab culture. They provided transportation and food for many desert peoples.

The Chinese saw chariot driver Wang Liang in the stars. Gamma Cassiopeiae was his whip. Wang Liang once drove for a hunter. Wang Liang drove correctly. But the hunter could not hit a single bird. The hunter was angry. He said Wang Liang was a bad driver. Wang Liang drove the hunter again. This time, the hunter hit 10 birds. He asked Wang Liang to be his driver full time. But Wang Liang refused.

Ancient Chinese chariots were pulled by horses.

On the second hunt, Wang Liang had driven differently. He drove the chariot in a way that made it easier for the hunter. He did not want to drive for a man who could only hunt by cheating.

The Native American Quileute people tell a story of five brothers hunting elk. An elk kills four of the brothers. But the fifth kills the elk. He uses five stakes to stretch the elk's skin. The stars show the holes he made. The Chukchi people of northeastern Russia see these stars as five reindeer in the river of the Milky Way.

CHAPTER FIVE

How to Find Cassiopeia in the Sky

Cassiopeia is always in the night sky for people in the Northern Hemisphere. To find her, face north. Look for the Little Dipper. The star at the tip of its handle is Polaris. Cassiopeia circles this star. Her W or M shape will be nearby.

Another useful trick is to look for the Big Dipper. It always sits across from Cassiopeia on the other side of Polaris. Trace a line from any star on the Big Dipper's handle through Polaris. This line points to Cassiopeia.

The vain queen does not often grace the skies of the Southern Hemisphere. But she can sometimes be seen there from October to December. Southern skywatchers should look for her M low on the horizon.

THE THREE GUIDES

Caph, the brightest star in Cassiopeia, has long been used to help find the North Star, Polaris. People on Earth use Polaris to find the direction north. Caph and two other stars are known as the Three Guides. Alpheratz is in Andromeda. Algenib is in Pegasus. These three stars mark an imaginary line that passes through Polaris.

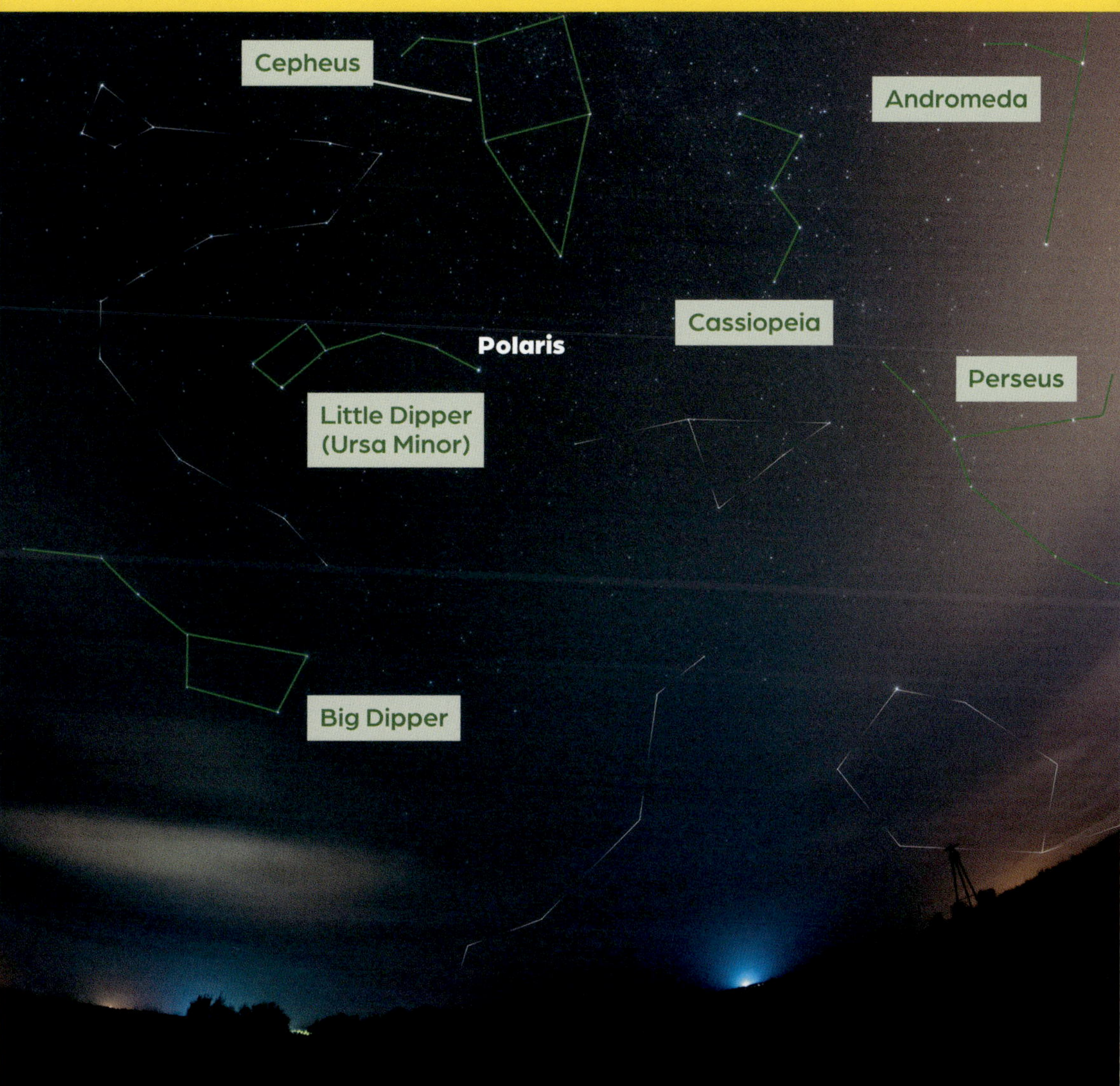

Cassiopeia is part of the Perseus Family of constellations.

GLOSSARY

ancient (AYN-shunt) Something that is ancient is very old or belongs to times long ago. Ancient Greeks told stories about Cassiopeia.

astronomer (uh-STRAW-nuh-mur) An astronomer is a scientist who studies stars and other objects in space. Ptolemy was an ancient astronomer.

chariot (CHAYR-ee-uht) A chariot is a small vehicle pulled by horses. Chinese astronomers saw the stars of Cassiopeia as chariot driver Wang Liang.

galaxy (GAL-uhk-see) A galaxy is a group of dust, gases, and billions of stars held together by gravity. Earth's galaxy is called the Milky Way.

gravity (GRA-vih-tee) Gravity is a force that pulls objects toward each other. Gravity pulls stars together to form star clusters.

hemisphere (HEH-mih-sfeer) A hemisphere is half of a sphere. Earth is divided into the Northern Hemisphere and Southern Hemisphere.

humble (HUM-bull) A person who is humble is not proud and does not feel more important than others. Cassiopeia was not humble.

oracle (OR-uh-kuhl) An oracle is a person who speaks for the gods and often can predict the future. King Cepheus went to an oracle for advice.

sacrifice (SAK-rih-fysse) To sacrifice something is to give it up for the sake of something more important. Cepheus and Cassiopeia were going to sacrifice their daughter to the sea monster to save the kingdom.

throne (THROHN) A throne is the chair of a queen or king. Cassiopeia's throne tips upside down in the sky.

universe (YOO-nih-vers) The universe is everything that exists in space. There are many stars in the universe.

vain (VAYN) A vain person is very proud, especially of their appearance. Cassiopeia was vain.

X-ray waves (EX-ray WAYVZ) X-ray waves are light rays that carry more energy than the light that humans can see. Cassiopeia A sends out X-ray waves visible with special telescopes.

FAST FACTS

- Constellations are groupings of stars in the sky that form pictures. Stars are glowing balls of gas throughout the universe. The Sun is a star.
- The constellation Cassiopeia is named for a queen from Greek mythology. Cassiopeia bragged about her beauty. The sea god Poseidon punished her by sending a flood and a sea monster. Cassiopeia and her husband, Cepheus, were forced to sacrifice their daughter, Andromeda, to the monster. But the hero Perseus saved Andromeda and the kingdom from the monster.
- Many cultures have stories for the stars in Cassiopeia. Arabs saw a hand, a camel, or a dog in the stars. Chinese astronomers saw a chariot.
- Cassiopeia has been recognized as a constellation for thousands of years.
- Cassiopeia is always in the sky in the Northern Hemisphere. People can find the constellation by finding Polaris, the North Star. When viewed facing north, Cassiopeia forms a W in the summer and an M in the winter.

ONE STRIDE FURTHER

- This book talked about space objects found in Cassiopeia. Which of these space objects do you find most interesting? Where could you find more information about space objects?
- Many cultures have stories about Cassiopeia. Do you have a favorite? Why? Where could you find out more information about your favorite story?
- Why did Poseidon choose to punish Cassiopeia? Do you think Cassiopeia deserved her punishment? Why or why not?

FIND OUT MORE

IN THE LIBRARY

Gibbons, Gail. *Stargazers*. New York, NY: Holiday House, 2023.

Harvey-Smith, Lisa. *Universal Guide to the Night Sky*. New York, NY: Thames & Hudson, 2024.

Read, John A. *A Kid's Guide to the Night Sky*. Naperville, IL: Sourcebooks, 2024.

ON THE WEB

Visit our website for links about Cassiopeia:

childsworld.com/links

Note to Parents, Caregivers, Teachers, and Librarians: We routinely verify our web links to make sure they are safe and active sites. So encourage your readers to check them out!

INDEX